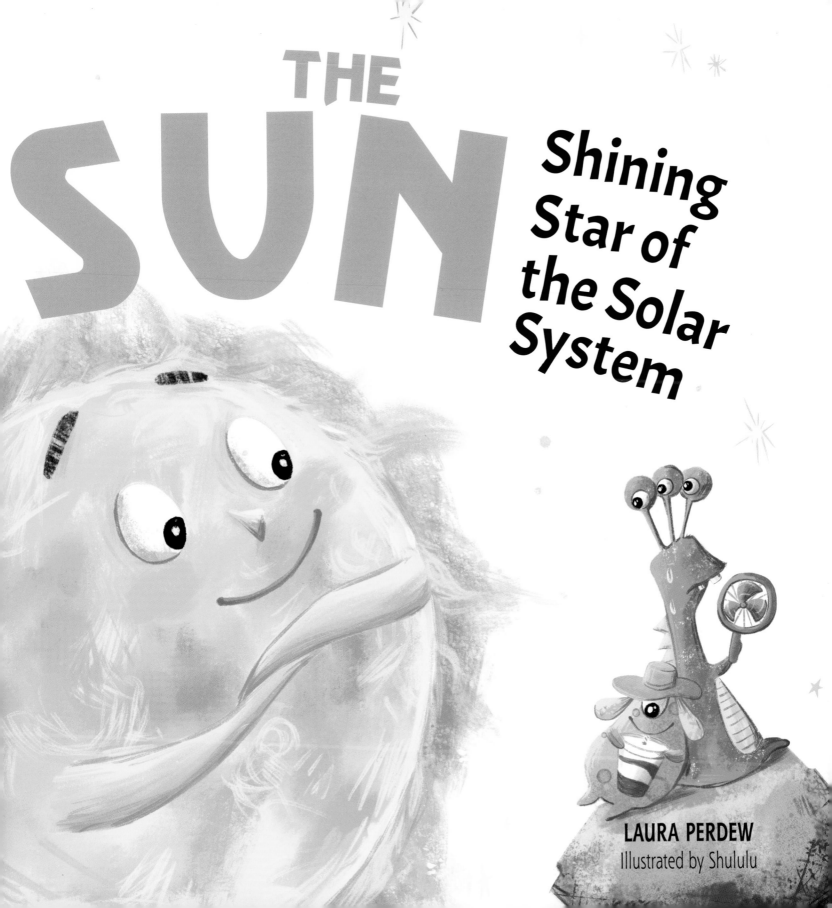

THE SUN

Shining Star of the Solar System

LAURA PERDEW

Illustrated by Shululu

SUN

Shining, hot, gassy.

Center of your solar system.

Sun loves keeping the planets in orbit

And is afraid of growing old, blinking out.

Sometimes calm, sometimes roiling,

Sun gives light, warmth, energy.

Sun is proud it gives life to Earth.

It creates auroras, eclipses, days and nights, seasons,

And hopes Earthlings will use its power.

Resident of the Milky Way galaxy.

A star.

Hello, Earthlings!

Universe here to tell you about one of my shining stars.

Your sun!

Yes, your sun is a star.

Literally.

It's happening again.

Yup. Universe is bragging about its awesomeness.

And while I have more stars than a sea otter has hairs, your sun plays the lead role in your solar system.

1

Let's start at the
very beginning.

As I grew from nothing into something and expanded,
I formed your solar system. That was about 4.5 billion years ago.

Yes, I'm very old. Yet, I've aged well.

At the center of that swirling, spinning disk
of a solar system, a star was born. Your sun.

Universe makes it sound so nice.

That messy star nursery was made of gas and dust!

It's called a solar nebula.

3

Your sun is one of hundreds of billions of stars in the Milky Way galaxy. And there are **A LOT** of other galaxies with billions of their own stars.

I know what you're thinking— that's so many stars! But in your solar system, your sun is the only one, so . . .

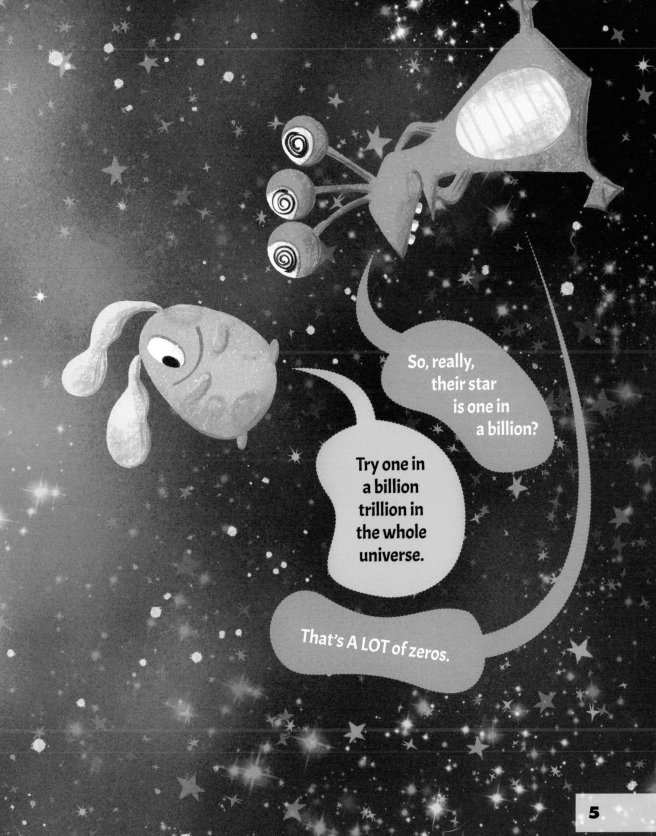

. . . I put it in charge.

Hey, I can't do **EVERYTHING!**

Your sun is up to the task. Using its gravity, the sun keeps all the planets and other space debris in your solar system in orbit.

MARS

EARTH

MERCURY

SATURN

Good thing, too!
If the sun didn't do its job, Earth and everything else would drift off into deep space!

JUPITER

VENUS

URANUS

NEPTUNE

Ha! Those Earthlings used to believe everything revolved around THEM, that they ruled the cosmic neighborhood.

Of course they did.

While your sun does a stellar job keeping everything in your solar system in line, as stars go, it's actually pretty average.

Sorry.

Many of my other stars are **BIGGER** and **BRIGHTER** than yours. Many are smaller.

Just like all the other stars, your sun is a
SUPER-hot,
gassy ball of
ENERGY.

9

Sometimes, its **boiling**, **roiling** surface is calm. Other times?

Watch out!

Your sun can be pretty violent. Like when it has those massive explosions of energy called solar flares.

Sometimes, it even burps out gas and particles into the solar system. **So rude.**

Luckily, Earth has a magnetic field around it that protects you people from those explosions and burps.

Your sun is still close enough to give you
warmth—not too much and not too little.
It also gives you energy. And light.

And that light you're seeing RIGHT NOW?

12

13

It started traveling from the sun
8 minutes ago!

Ancient Earthlings used that light to tell time. When your side of the Earth faces the sun,
it's daytime.
And when you are facing away,
it's nighttime.

Do you know why?

Because your planet is spinning.

It makes one full rotation in 24 hours.

That's an Earth day!

If one rotation of Earth is one day, what makes one Earth year?

One orbit of the Earth around the sun.

MERCURY

EARTH

NEPTUNE

16

On Earth, that's 365 days.

If you lived on one of my other planets, such as Mercury, your year might only be 88 days.

Or one year might be 165 Earth years on Neptune!

Guess what else your sun controls?

SEASONS!

Earth is tilted on its axis. When the North Pole points toward the sun, the Northern Hemisphere has summer.

The days are **loooooong and warm**, thanks to the sun.

Then, Earth moves around the sun and the South Pole points more toward the sun.

That's when **it's winter up north** and **summer in the south**.

Here's the best part—all that
light and warmth and energy is
why you have life on Earth.

Plants use the sun's energy
for photosynthesis.

Animals—including you—depend
on plants for food and oxygen.

The sun keeps everything warm, too. That
star of yours is why you have liquid water.
And all life on your planet needs water!

If all that wasn't incredible enough, your sun puts on a **REALLY COOL** light show for you Earthlings, too. Remember when I told you that the sun spews out energy and particles into space?

When those solar particles interact with your atmosphere, they create auroras. **THEY'RE BEAUTIFUL!**

23

Your sun also plays a starring
role in eclipses. When I send
the moon right between
the sun and your Earth,
there's a solar eclipse.

When that happens, the moon
blocks out the sun's light and
casts a shadow on Earth. So, even
though it's the middle of the day,
the sky gets dark for a while.

25

Your sun really is pretty incredible, if I do say so myself. And I'm happy to see that you clever Earthlings have also finally figured out how to put the sun's endless energy to work on Earth. You have a star among you—its new role supplying clean energy is sure to be a blockbuster!

Make a Model of the
Solar System

The sun is at the center of our solar system. All the planets and other objects orbit around it in their own paths.

Aurora borealis

WHAT YOU NEED

various sized balls, Styrofoam balls, pom-poms or construction paper circles, string, glue, large black posterboard

WHAT YOU DO

First, ask an adult to help you research the solar system and the planets in it. Select balls or circle cutouts to represent each of the eight planets and the sun, based on their sizes. For example, the sun will be the largest object. Mercury will be the smallest (and VERY small compared to the sun).

Place the planets in orbit around the sun in the correct order. You might place the balls on the floor or hang them from the ceiling. Or you could paste cutouts on a large piece of black paper. Which planet is closest to the sun? Which planet is farthest away?

What other objects in our solar system can you include in your model? How about our moon or an asteroid belt? Where might a comet go? You might even want to include Pluto in your model!

Glossary

artial solar eclipse

atmosphere: a blanket of gases around the earth.

asteroid belt: a collection of small, rocky objects that orbit the sun between Mars and Jupiter.

aurora: a colorful light show caused by particles from solar winds colliding with the earth's atmosphere.

axis: the imaginary line around which the earth rotates.

comet: a ball of ice and dust that orbits the sun.

coronal mass ejection: when the sun sends bursts of gas and particles into space.

debris: the pieces left after something has been destroyed.

eclipse: when an object in space is blocked by another object, causing a shadow.

equator: an imaginary line around the earth, halfway between the North and South Poles.

galaxy: a collection of star systems held together by gravity.

gravity: a force that pulls objects toward each other and all objects to the earth.

magnetic field: a force field created by the earth's core that protects the planet from the sun's strong energy.

Milky Way: the galaxy that contains our solar system.

Northern Hemisphere: the half of the earth north of the equator.

orbit: the path a planet travels around the sun.

oxygen: a gas in the air that animals and humans need to breathe to stay alive.

photosynthesis: how plants turn sunlight and water into food to grow.

planet: a large body in space that orbits the sun and does not produce its own light. There are eight planets.

revolve: to turn or spin around a central point.

rotate: to turn around a fixed point.

solar flare: a sudden burst of energy from the sun's surface.

solar nebula: a collection of dust and gas that eventually forms a solar system.

solar particle: a tiny piece of matter from the sun.

solar system: a family of eight planets and their moons that orbit the sun.

star: an astronomical body that makes its own light.

universe: everything that exists, everywhere.

Sunlight on earth

A solar flare

29

SPARK SCIENTIFIC CURIOSITY WITH THIS PICTURE BOOK SCIENCE SET!

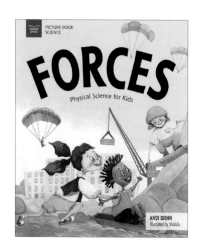

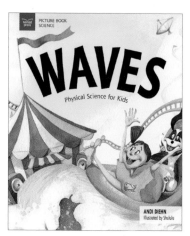

Check out more titles at www.nomadpress.net

Nomad Press

A division of Nomad Communications

10 9 8 7 6 5 4 3 2 1

This book was manufactured by CGB Printers,
North Mankato, Minnesota, United States
March 2021, Job #1018010

ISBN Softcover: 978-1-61930-980-7
ISBN Hardcover: 978-1-61930-977-7

Educational Consultant, Marla Conn

Questions regarding the ordering of this book should be addressed to
Nomad Press
2456 Christian St., White River Junction, VT 05001
www.nomadpress.net

Printed in the United States.